SMART GREEN CIVILIZATIONS

ANCIENT CHINA

teri

The Energy and Resources Institute

A note from Dr R K Pachauri

Human civilization in its race towards progress has at times ignored its adverse effects on nature. With every passing century, man has intensified his quest for a tomorrow better than today, and issues like environment-friendly living, usage of clean energy and preventing the harmful effects of chemicals on nature are becoming increasingly important. Contrary to popular belief, these can be tackled without compromising on our comforts. All we need to do is turn a few pages of history and relearn lessons that civilizations from various parts of the world have left behind.

This series provides a unique and interesting perspective of history from the eyes of an environmentalist. It highlights the environmental wisdom of ancient people. These books bring alive ancient civilizations and their simple, earth-friendly lifestyles—building bright and airy houses from mud bricks, using the sun's energy to heat homes, utilizing plants to make natural dyes, applying manure to grow crops, and many more such techniques.

Exploring the fascinating civilizations of the ancient world and bringing forth little known 'green lessons' from the past, I hope these books will ensure that young readers put to use the knowledge of yesteryears to lay the foundation for a prosperous future.

R K Pachauri
Director-General, TERI
Chairman, Intergovernmental Panel on Climate Change

Contents

Teri goes to ancient China

The history of human settlements in China goes back more than 16,000 years. However, the oldest human fossil in China was found in Shanxi province, and dates back to 600,000 BC! China is one of the oldest civilizations in the world. It is also one of the few civilizations to survive from ancient times to the present. China's location is one reason for this.

This vast land has almost all geographical formations, from forests to mountains, deserts, lakes and coastal plains to grasslands and plateaus. To its east are the China Sea and the Yellow Sea. While these kept raiders at bay, the mighty Himalaya mountains to the south and west acted like a wall.

HIMALAYAS

Wow… a Chinese dragon! I read in my history lesson that a dragon is a sign of good luck.

Later, at night…

Don't be scared Teri, I'm here to take you to an ancient land that is still flourishing today.

S-H-R-I-E-K!!!

Off to the land of dragons and emperors!!!

▶ The oldest surviving civilization in the world, ancient China was ruled by a series of emperors from different dynasties. Isolated from the rest of the world, not only by geographical features, but also by the imposing Great Wall, the Chinese are known for their inventions and technological advancements.

GREEN GEM Trade through the Takla Makan Desert would have been impossible but for oasis towns like Kashgar, Niya, and Khotan. These towns got water after rains hit the surrounding mountains.

To the north, the Gobi Desert kept enemies away. To the west was the dry Takla Makan Desert, home to poisonous snakes and insects. Some believe its name means, 'if you go there, you don't come out alive'. That is why it is also called the Sea of Death. The only raiders to attack China were the Mongol tribes from Central Asia.

Little is known about the early rulers of China. The first dynasty we know of was the Xia, which ruled from about the twenty-first to the sixteenth century BC. The Chinese civilization has given the world many firsts. This includes the compass, paper, silk, printing, fireworks, wheelbarrows, and even the tea your parents drink!

GOBI DESERT

TAKLA MAKAN DESERT

GREAT WALL

BEIJING

SUZHOU

XINING

YANGZHOU

PLATEAU OF TIBET

LUOYANG

XIAN

RIVER YANGTZE

CHENGDU

SHANGHAI

LHASA

NANNING

YELLOW SEA

and NOW

The ancient Chinese were known for their many useful inventions. Even today, Chinese goods and products are exported to all parts of the world.

The way they lived

Society in ancient China was divided into the rich upper class and the poor class. People were also divided into different social classes according to their occupation and status. There were four major classes—scholars, farmers, artisans, and traders.

Scholars were highly respected, as few others had knowledge. Below the aristocratic scholars were farmers. They not only produced food for the people, but also earned income for the country, and were respected landowners. Craftsmen and artisans represented the labour class. They did not own land, but helped in production and often ran their own business. Traders comprised the fourth class. They used the Silk Road— the ancient trade route that linked China with Europe—to trade in silk, perfume, cosmetics, clothing fabrics, herbs, and medicines.

Where have we landed?

Welcome! You are in ancient China. I'm Confucius, your teacher and guide.

▼ Artisans and craftsmen had skills and worked hard to make useful objects. Their skills were handed down from father to son.

◄ Merchants earned a lot of money, but they were not respected as much as scholars and farmers.

▼ Farmers were considered valuable members of society, as they produced food for the people.

◄ Scholars were highly respected because of their knowledge.

The Chinese regarded the family as the most important part of society. People lived in joint families. Three or four generations lived together. The oldest person ran the house. Each home had an altar to pay respect to dead ancestors, so that they blessed the home.

Most children did not study in schools, but worked on their parents' farms. Only boys of rich families studied at home or went to a tutor. They were taught literature, science, mathematics, art, music, as well as the teachings of wise people like Confucius. Girls did not go to school. They were married at a young age, after which they had to leave their parents' homes. Women did household work and had to respect the men.

and NOW

THEN

The ancient Chinese believed in discipline, concentration, and power. Around 2600 BC, Emperor Huang Di encouraged troops to learn martial arts. Disciplines like Tai Chi are still practised for good health.

Innovative farmers

Like most civilizations, ancient China depended on agriculture. Most settlements were along the rivers. Rivers like the Yangtze Kiang flooded every year, depositing a fertile yellow soil called loess on the banks.

When people realized that loess helped plants to grow, they began to farm in these areas. The Chinese were among the first to grow rice and hemp, as early as 6000 BC. They planted rice in the floodplains, as rice needs standing water. Rice was the main food crop. It was also made into wine. They grew wheat, barley, sorghum, and millet, fruit and vegetables, including gourds, acorns, nuts, beans, and water chestnuts. Farmers reared buffaloes and pigs.

Is this a see-saw for kids?

Aha...now that is one of the many clever tools we Chinese invented. It was used to grind grain.

▼ The chain pump was a type of water pump with a series of discs on a chain. This device was operated by foot and was used to draw up water for irrigation.

Chinese farmers came up with many new ideas. Growing crops year after year made the soil poor, so they rested the soil for one season before cultivating it again. They understood that each crop drew out different nutrients from the soil, so they rotated the crops. In crop rotation, different crops were planted on the same land one after the other to make the soil fertile. Hemp was switched with adzuki beans. Soybean was grown, as the roots of this crop added nitrogen to the soil. Thousands of years later, it is still grown in China.

After harvesting, plants were ploughed into the soil as green manure. Chinese farmers wasted nothing. About 3,000 years ago, they used animal and human dung as fertilizer. They burnt weeds and spread the ash, while bones of dead animals were treated with ash and lime and added to the soil to help crops grow. Farmers made their work simpler with hoes, axes, and knives of bone and stone.

▲ Over 2,000 years ago, Chinese farmers used auto-irrigation, in which a covered earthen pot full of water was buried in a pit. The water seeped into the soil, helping the seeds to grow.

◄ The tilt hammer was a simple device in which the whole weight of the body was used for treading on it to pound grain.

THEN and NOW

As more and more parts of the world face water shortage, scientists are teaching farmers the ancient Chinese method of clay pot auto-irrigation.

10-11

Ancient cuisine

The Chinese have always been noted for their cuisine, or style of food preparation. Most of the dishes were made from rice or wheat. The ancient Chinese knew the art of food processing. Historians believe that one of the most popular foods today—noodles—was first made in China.

Dim sum was a type of traditional cuisine, in which small portions of a variety of foods, including steamed or fried dumplings, were served one after the other. Dumplings and other food were steamed over boiling water and flavoured with spices like ginger, garlic, and anise. They ate fish and different kinds of meat like pork, lamb, and chicken.

Mmm...all this talk of food has made me hungry.

I hope you can use chopsticks!

▶ Dim sums were important in Chinese meals. 'Dim sum' means, touch the heart. By the tenth century AD, the Chinese made about 2,000 types of dim sums!

◀ Chopsticks, called Kuai Zi, meaning 'small piece pickers', have been used in China since the Shang dynasty (1500–600 BC) in the Bronze Age.

◀ Archaeologists have found a bowl of thin yellow millet noodles at Lajia in north-west China, which could be as much as 4,000 years old. These are the world's oldest noodles!

The Chinese people have been using chopsticks to eat their food for more than 3,000 years. Chopsticks were made of wood, metal, bone or stone. Bamboo and wood chopsticks are still the most popular today.

Tea was discovered by the ancient Chinese around 2737 BC. This happened when the emperor was on a trip and his drinking water was being boiled to make it clean. Some dry tea leaves fell into the water and turned it brown, but the emperor found it very refreshing! Thus, the Chinese began to drink 'cha', or tea, several times a day. They even used it as a medicine to flush out toxins from the body. Tea was grown across the country and exported to South and West Asia. Tea and dim sums are still served together in China!

THEN and NOW
For centuries, tea has been taken as a digestive. Today, tea drinkers are warned that they may be drinking harmful pesticides with their tea, which could make them ill.

12-13

I'm what I wear

The earliest people in China kept themselves warm with animal skins. Then, they learnt to grow, spin, and weave fabric from hemp, ramie, and silk. It is believed that the Mongols brought cotton to China when they raided it around the thirteenth century. About 18,000 years ago, the Chinese made needles of bone and began to stitch clothes. For thousands of years, people in China wore long, loose robes or tunics with wide sleeves. In colder places, a quilted jacket was worn over that.

As society progressed, clothing was guided by strict rules made in court. Only the emperor could wear yellow. Silk and bright colours were for the rich. Some rulers passed orders that workers could wear only blue or black. The length of the tunic indicated the person's status. The rich, who did little work, wore them long over trousers. Common people wore simple tunics and pants, hats, and straw sandals. In winter, they wore padded coats or simply stuffed paper and cloth inside their jackets!

▶   The art of silk making has not changed much since ancient times. Silkworm cocoons were boiled in water, which separated the long silk filaments. These were turned into one thread by means of a spinning wheel.

How do I look?

In these bright, long robes, you look like a Chinese noble lady!

China taught the world to make silk from silkworm. Silk weaving and embroidery also started in China. It is believed that in 2700 BC, Empress Lei Zu discovered silk when the cocoon of a silkworm moth fell from a mulberry tree into her tea. She realized that silk filaments could be separated by dipping the cocoon into hot water. The filaments were made into yarn and spun into silk. Some of the oldest silk, dating back about 2,500 years, was found in a tomb in Jiangxi. Traders took Chinese silk across Asia to Europe along the ancient Silk Road.

▶ Women wore long tunics that reached down to the ground. Generally, both men and women kept their hair long. They believed that hair came from parents, so it was disrespectful to cut it.

and NOW

The ancient Chinese dyed fabric in plant colours. Blue was from indigo, while yellow was from gardenia. Hazel bark dyed cloth black, and red was from madder. Modern chemical dyes are harmful. Most do not last as long as natural dyes.

14-15

The walled empire

So many kings, so many dynasties... what kept you safe?

My dear, look at that huge wall...it kept invaders at bay.

From time immemorial to AD 1911, China has been ruled by emperors. Generally, there was a succession of rulers from the same family, called dynasty. The earliest written records are from the Shang dynasty in the thirteenth century BC. The longest dynasty was the Zhou (1066–221 BC).

First Emperor Ch'in Shih Huang Ti brought most of China together with one system of writing and the same weights and measures everywhere. He made strict laws and did not allow anyone to complain against the ruler.

The Shang dynasty (1500–600 BC) built the capital at Zhengdou, surrounded by about six kilometres of walls. Kong-Fuzi, or Confucius (551–479 BC), was adviser to the Zhou kings. He told the emperor to be kind and asked people to obey their ruler and respect their ancestors. His thoughts influenced China for more than 2,000 years.

The Han dynasty (206 BC–220 AD) saw the most progress. Emperors like Gaozu, founder of the dynasty, believed in the teachings of Confucius. People were encouraged to study.

◀ The First Emperor was buried with an entire army made of terracotta, or burnt earth. About 700,000 workers built this tomb, which was discovered only in 1974. The emperor began building this tomb when he was thirteen, so that he could rule again after his death!

GREEN GEM Chinese rulers like the Shang kings laid out beautifully landscaped gardens. Such gardens became popular among scholars, who used to sit quietly in these gardens and study nature.

During the Han period, scientists designed watermills and pumps, which helped farmers irrigate their fields.

Various dynasties built the Great Wall of China to protect their empire. It was built over 1,700 years, mainly to keep out Mongol raiders. Construction began during the Qin dynasty around 221 BC under Emperor Qin Shi Huangdi. He ordered slaves to build the wall with mud and stones fitted into wooden frames. The wall was also a watchtower. Most of the wall was made later, during the Ming dynasty (1388–1644 AD).

◄ The Great Wall is the only man-made structure visible from space. It is spread over 8,850 kilometres, though it is not continuous. In places, it is 4.5–9 metres thick. At its highest point, it is about 7.5 metres.

THEN and NOW
China gets its name from the Ch'in dynasty. After Communism replaced dynastic rule, the country was named the People's Republic of China.

16-17

Built to last

The earliest people in China lived in caves. Later, they made huts of wood and mud. Since wood does not last, we know about them from clay replicas used at funerals.

The poor lived in one-roomed thatched houses made of mud bricks. The rich had bigger houses with earthen walls. Palaces and houses of the rich followed the teachings of Taoism and Feng Shui (the art of arrangement). So, both sides of a house were identical to keep the energy in balance. Sloping roofs curved at the ends and rested on columns. There was stress on keeping bad spirits out and encouraging good luck.

Is this a town?

No, this is one of our grand palaces.

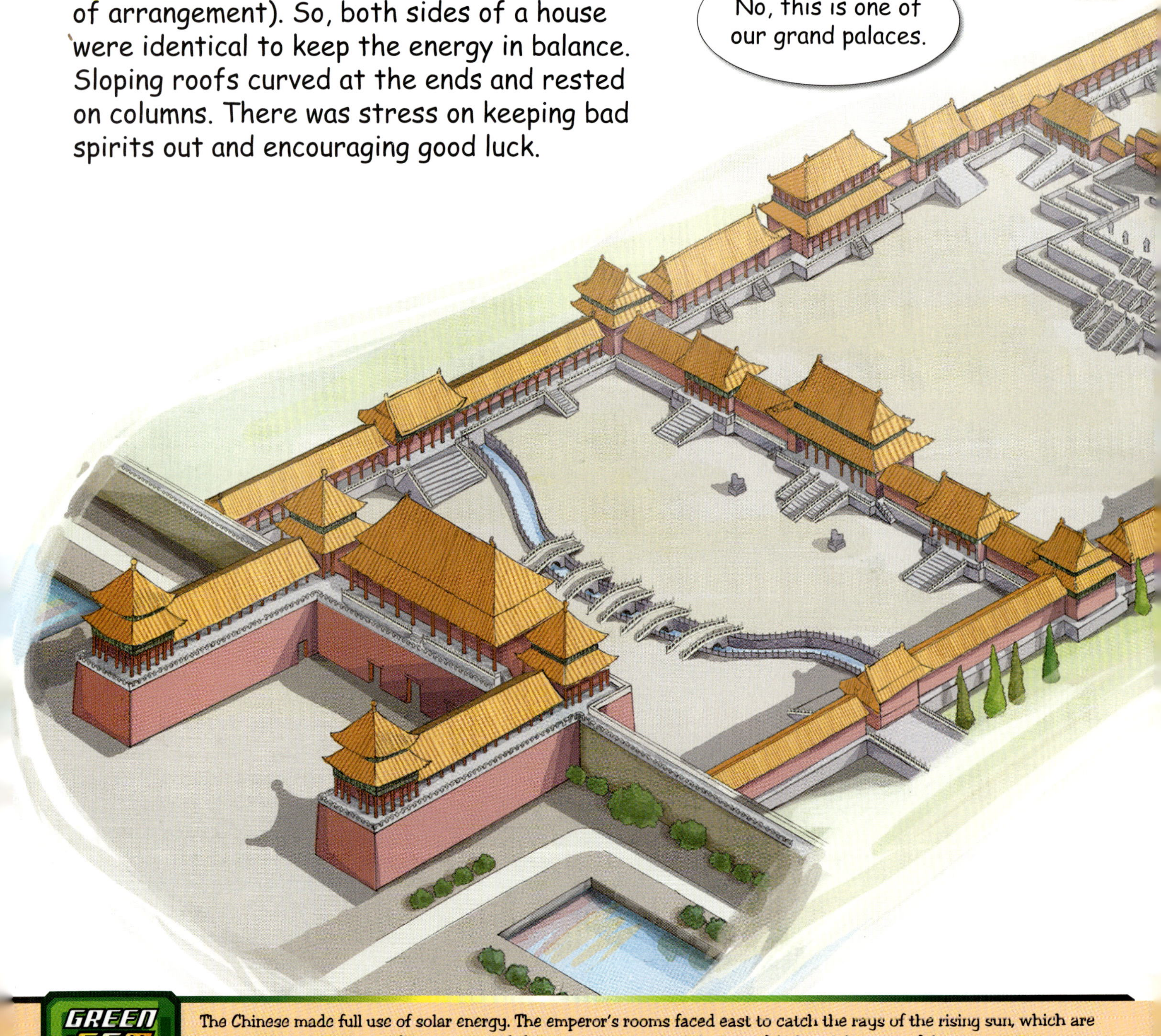

The Chinese made full use of solar energy. The emperor's rooms faced east to catch the rays of the rising sun, which are more healthy than those of the sun at mid-day or at sunset, when the harmful ultraviolet rays of the sun are strongest.

Chinese buildings were often built around open courtyards. These open spaces kept houses airy and cool. In the sunnier south, the courtyards were smaller to keep sunlight out. Carved overhangs on the south shielded windows from the summer sun. In the colder north, the courtyards and windows opened to the south to get the most sunshine and keep out the cold northerly breeze. There were hardly any windows opening to the north, west or east. Windows had wooden lattices covered with silk or paper to block the wind and let in sunlight.

At the centre of the house was the family shrine with living rooms on the sides. Common walls were built to keep several houses safe from robbers and floodwaters. Buildings were built according to strict laws. Only people from royal families could build a house with ten columns.

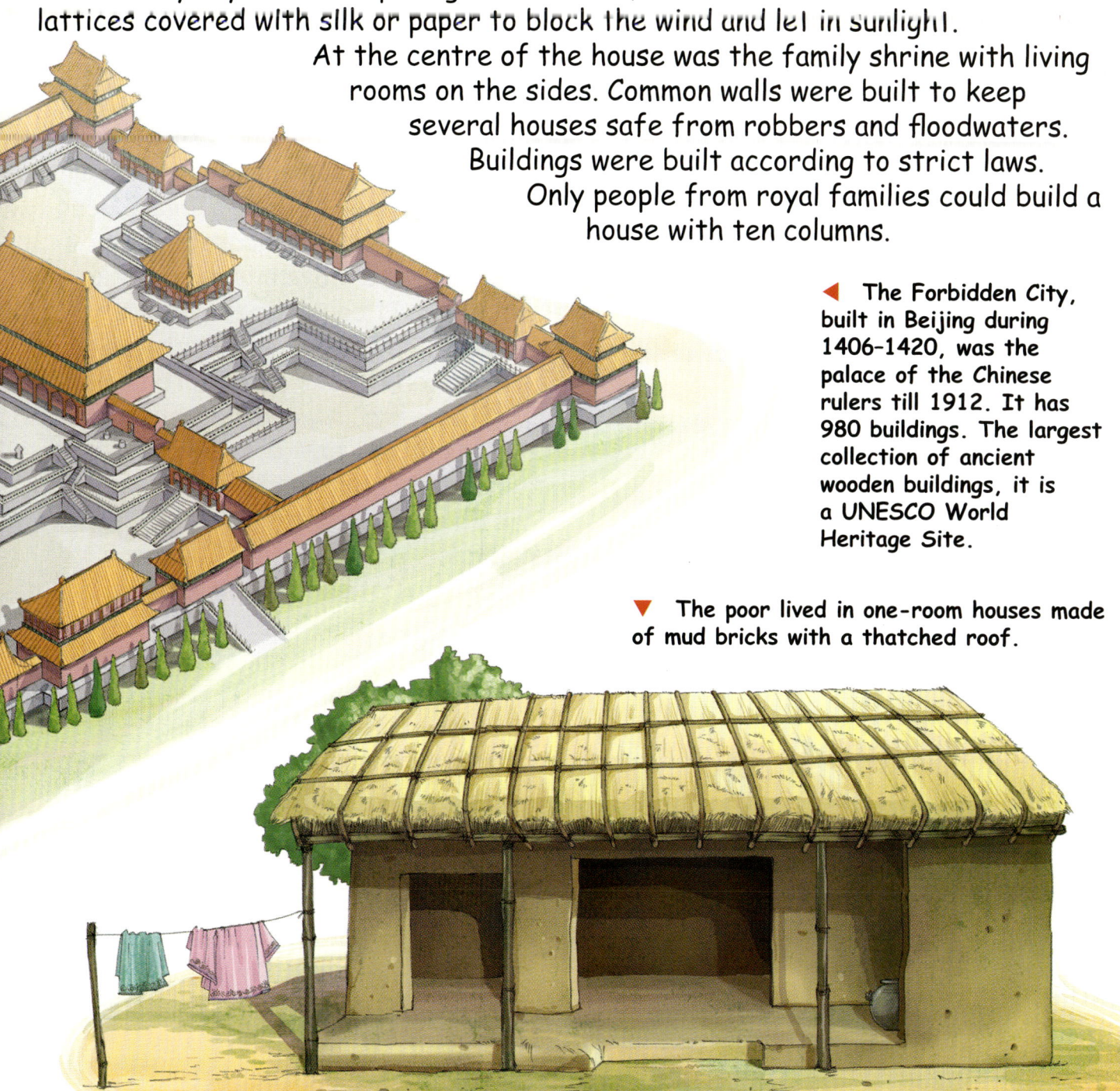

◄ The Forbidden City, built in Beijing during 1406–1420, was the palace of the Chinese rulers till 1912. It has 980 buildings. The largest collection of ancient wooden buildings, it is a UNESCO World Heritage Site.

▼ The poor lived in one-room houses made of mud bricks with a thatched roof.

THEN and NOW

Many ancient Chinese buildings made of mud bricks still stand today. Modern buildings, made of bricks and steel, often fail to withstand China's major earthquakes. In May 2008, over five million people lost their homes after a major earthquake.

18-19

Oh, it's raining!

Here, take this umbrella, another ancient Chinese invention!

Ancient science and wisdom

The Chinese have contributed a lot to science, technology, mathematics, astronomy, and medicine. Many of their inventions had a big impact on the world. While the abacus and the shadow clock were among the earliest inventions, ancient China is most noted for its four great inventions—the magnetic compass, gunpowder, paper-making, and printing.

Ancient Chinese scientist Zhang Heng invented the first seismograph in AD 132, a useful device in earthquake-prone China. It could measure wind movements and warn of an earthquake. The first earthquake it detected pointed east. Some days later, a messenger from the east arrived to report that there had indeed been an earthquake.

The Chinese were keenly interested in medicine. Around 202 BC, Zhang Zhongjing wrote a book on tackling colds. Surgeons like Hua Tuo (AD 140–208) made anaesthetics from wine and cannabis. This made the patient unconscious of the pain during the surgery. Doctors used traditional Chinese medicine of herbs and animal parts to cure various ailments.

Emperor Huang-ti encouraged the study of mathematics. His ministers Li-shou and Tai-mao worked out a system of numbers that was written vertically.

▼ Ancient Chinese doctors discovered the medicinal effects of thousands of herbs over a long period of time.

▲ Around the third century BC, the Chinese invented the magnetic compass. This helped them find their way both on land and over sea. It is still used widely to find direction.

Zu Chongzhi and his son Zu Gengzhi wrote the mathematical book *Zhui Shu* and made several accurate astronomical calculations.

The Chinese built the first planetarium to study the stars. They were the first to record observations of comets and solar eclipses. But although they observed solar eclipses, they believed a dragon had swallowed the sun.

▼ This ancient seismograph, decorated with dragons and frogs, had a copper ball inside, which dropped out from the mouth of one dragon and fell into the mouth of the frog below. There were eight dragons representing eight directions. From the direction of the falling ball, it was judged where an earthquake might happen.

THEN and NOW

Chinese astronomer, mathematician, and engineer Zu Chongzhi had no modern machines to calculate, but he calculated that a year was made up of 365.24281481 days. Today, we know a year has 365.24219878 days.

Time to spare

What's that? Are you doing magic tricks?

No, that's shadow puppetry, an ancient form of storytelling and entertainment.

Many of the board games we play began in China. Go, called Yi in ancient China, was played on a grid with seventeen rows and columns. The oldest known board game, it was played by two players. It probably began in about 2350 BC, when Emperor Yao ordered the designing of a game that would make his boisterous son Danzhu concentrate. Other board games were designed to train soldiers in battlefield strategies. The puzzle ring is believed to have been designed during the Warring States Age (476–221 BC). It has nine intertwined rings that have to be separated. Some say, the Chinese general Hung Ming designed it in the second century for his wife. He thought she would be busy trying to solve it and would not miss him while he was at war.

The Chinese were expert potters. They made porcelain, a fine pottery, in special kilns that could work at very high temperatures. Lacquer was made into jewellery, statues, utensils, and boxes. They painted beautiful scrolls in the typical Chinese style of painting and carved jade. Fond of the arts, they tied cords into beautiful knots that had religious meaning.

◄ Amongst the oldest of the instruments used in China were the Chinese flutes, while the pipa was a popular instrument used to create soothing melodies.

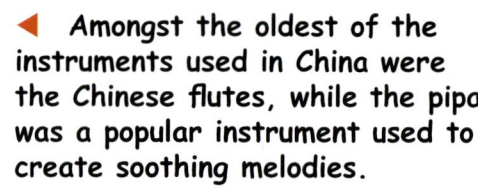

GREEN GEM Almost 3,000 years ago, the first kites were made in China using silk and bamboo. They were also used for checking wind direction, communicating during war, and even calculating distance. Today, kites are often made of non-biodegradable plastic.

▲ Go was a board game of encirclement and capture that remains popular even today.

▼ It was Chinese potters who began making porcelain, a highly refined form of pottery making. This art was developed over many years, and later, China became known for its high-quality porcelain, or 'china'.

Some of the world's earliest music was played in China. Archaeologists have found six flutes made of the bone of the red-crowned crane at Jiahu, in Henan province. These are about 9,000 years old. By 433 BC, Chinese musicians made transverse flutes out of bamboo. Children played with rattles, and whistles of clay and bamboo. They were entertained with shadow puppets.

and NOW

The Chinese gave the world the tangram, a seven-piece puzzle. The tangram has been used in designing furniture and even in modern art.

Travel and trade

The ancient Chinese mostly travelled on foot. Wealthy people rode horses. Nobles also used litter vehicles, or vehicles carried by people or animals. By the time of the Han dynasty (206–220 BC), litters, or jiao, were seats made of bamboo and carried on a person's back. People also used ox-drawn carts.

By the start of the Song dynasty in AD 960, the palanquin was common. Brides were carried to their new homes in a shoulder carriage coloured red with lacquer, and decorated with gold paint and silk curtains.

The Chinese were among the earliest people to make maps. The oldest map found dates to the fourth century BC.

Wow, I want to take a ride on that carriage!

That's a jiao...it was carried by people.

◄ The ancient Chinese palanquin was made of bamboo and decorated with curtains. It was carried by four bearers.

China had enough to trade with other countries, sending out silk and bringing in gold. Traders took the Silk Road, linking China to India, Uzbekistan, and Persia. Traders went as far west as Italy, 4,000 miles away. Chinese traders carried ivory, silk, and spices and brought back gold, gems, and glass. The route was difficult. It crossed deserts that were blistering hot during the day and bitterly cold at night. They lumbered over mountains with their goods and had to dodge bandits and snakes.

Over land and by sea, China traded with many countries along the Silk Road. These included Myanmar, Thailand, India, Iraq, Iran, and Egypt. Instead of money, the first traders used cowrie shells. Bronze coins were used around 400 BC and paper money, around AD 1100.

By about 220 BC, Chinese shipbuilders made hardy ships called junks. Such ships are still used today.

▲▼ The Chinese invented the wheelbarrow. The early ones had a single wheel in the middle. Farmers and builders used the wheelbarrow to carry heavy loads, while soldiers used it to remove injured or dead people from the battlefield. Later wheelbarrows had two wheels.

THEN and NOW

The ancient Chinese sailing ships called junks had four to six enormous sails. Flat and easy to handle, the design of these sails are considered so efficient that they are still used in sailboats.

The write way

Oh, no...my hands are stained with ink!

Don't worry...that ink will not harm you. It does not contain chemicals.

The Chinese began writing between 1500 BC and 600 BC, under the Shang dynasty. They used pictograms, or symbols that signify a word. Pictograms were an effective way of recording facts. The ancient Chinese secret scroll found in Weng in northern China lists, in just 1,500 words, all the wells and eating outlets in Weng. This was the start of calligraphy, the art of Chinese writing. It was written with a brush and black ink. Although calligraphy is now popular in many languages, it began in China. The angular Chinese characters were written like beautiful images.

The ancient Chinese wrote on bones and on tortoise shells. Oracle bones were tools to look into the future. One of the first major writings in ancient China was the *I Ching*, or *Book of Changes*, a book on predictions. They also wrote on sheets of bamboo and silk.

FISH

RAIN

CLOUD

SUN

◀ Early Chinese script contained 80,000 different characters.

Paper was first made in China by mixing the bark of a mulberry tree and bamboo fibres with water. The mixture was drained and dried on a flat bamboo frame to make sheets.

The Chinese were the first to invent paper and printing. Around AD 100, they invented paper from mulberry and hemp pulp. Since paper was easier to make than silk, it proved cheaper, and more books began to be printed. It also made more silk available for export. Around AD 700, the Chinese were the first to use wooden blocks to print text. By AD 1000, the movable clay type was ready. This led to the production of books. Book shops opened in cities, and more people began to study. The first libraries were built around temples and in palaces.

▲ Boiling the bamboo after it was ground and soaked in lime to make it soft.

▶ Straining the boiled and washed bamboo.

◀ Flattening and drying the sheets.

THEN and **NOW**

Some of the earliest Chinese pictograms are still used in the Japanese Kanji alphabet.

26-27

Marching ahead

China is an ancient civilization that was never wiped out. It is now the most populous country and among the most powerful nations in the world. It has large industries producing goods that are sold all over the world. To run its growing industries, China needs more and more power. There are huge power plants and dams. The largest is the Three Gorges Dam across the Yangtze river.

However, large-scale development has also caused damage to the environment. For example, the building of the Three Gorges Dam has wiped out the Yangtze river dolphin. It has left the Siberian crane critically endangered because the wetlands, once its home, were inundated by the dam. China has the rare and unique Chinese alligator, and snub-nosed golden monkey. In the last century, animals like the South China tiger were hunted as pests. The tiger was almost driven to extinction by the time hunting was banned in 1977.

▶ China is an ancient country developing into a modern power.

A growing China!

The giant panda is the most famous of Chinese wild animals. It lives in the mountains of central and south-west China. It feeds totally on bamboo and can eat fourteen kilograms of bamboo shoots a day. With growing human population, more and more forests have been cleared for farming, cities, and other projects, leaving little space and food for the panda. The ancient Chinese believed the panda was a noble creature but it has been poached for centuries for its fur. Some years ago, it was in danger of becoming extinct. Today, with care, the numbers are rising.

Yes, by leaps and bounds....

THEN and NOW

China had started losing its forest cover due to deforestation and other human activities, but now, it is one of the few countries that have been rapidly increasing their forest cover. It has also reduced air and water pollution.

Green lessons

- Ancient Chinese buildings were built according to the climate—in warm areas, they kept the sun out; in colder areas, they were built to get the most sunshine and keep out the cold breeze.

- Chinese farmers wasted nothing and used natural manure like animal and human dung. They also adopted new methods like clay pot auto-irrigation to use water wisely for irrigation.

- The ancient Chinese dyed fabric in plant colours.

- While cooking, portions of food were chopped small to save fuel and time.